DIFFERENT SPHERES OF LIFE

KOPPARA AADITYA PATNAIK

ISBN 979-888530805-2

<u>*Different spheres of life*</u>

Preface :-

"Different spheres of life " gives us an insight into the various colours of life. These are short poems based on the different perspectives of life .

From sadness to exuberance, it gives us an insight into almost every aspect of the epistemology of life.

Life is a beautiful gift by God to us.

Having a life means you have a chance to achieve what you want, enjoy things and live with people around you.

Many of us don't understand the importance of Life and thus spend most of our lives in regret.

Life is not all about pain and regret, but about the experiences and learnings, we have.

The best thing about Life is that it keeps moving forward.

No matter what happens in our lives at one point, our life keeps moving and so we should also learn to move on in our life without any regrets.

Whatever happens in life, it happens for a reason.

So, instead of blaming our circumstances, we should understand the reason behind it and enjoy every aspect of life.

Survival of mankind without nature is impossible and humans need to understand that.

If nature has the ability to protect us, it is also powerful enough to destroy the entire mankind.

Every form of nature, for instance, the plants, animals, rivers, mountains, moon, and more holds equal significance for us.

All of these ideologies are compressed into this one book!!!!!!!!!!!!!!!

<u>Different spheres of life</u>

-Koppara Aaditya Patnaik

<u>Contents:-</u>

Boulevard of broken dreams:-

I walk alone

on the boulevard of broken dreams

Living on a loan

living on day dreams

I don't know where it goes

but it's home to me

and I walk alone

on it's lonely streets.

The little one:-

Far away a little tiger

Stays awake all night

Wandering around

With its innocent eyes

Filled with tears

It's scared away by the giants

Thirsty during the day

Wet at night

Under the heavy rain

It sleeps into its memories

Thinking about Its mother

Afraid and all alone.

A spark:-

A sudden spark

Fell on the cracker

It busted into flames

And flew into the river

Blinded by the sparks

I still saw beautiful colours

So black and fair

Two gorgeous mood changing discolours.

The wings of freedom:-

It was at one spring-sunset

When the little one came out

Scared and shivering

Working on a spread-out

It opened its wings

Took a sigh

And then jumped

It fell down

Almost

When suddenly it rouse towards the sun

Unknowingly though

Because it was lost in the cold breeze

It was flying

In a freeze

Widening its wings

Wings of freedom

A mother :-

It Saw its child's wings

Turn into the wings of fire

Taking their swings

She was cursed with

This blessing

Proud and contended

with this happening.

A treasure:-

A special treasure

Unknown at first

A key

To unlock a child's mind

Like a shepherd

Guiding the sheep

A sample book

For the student

Containing the answer key

For the student's life's trial

Thank you Teachers

For all you have done

In the group of many

You are a special one.

Time:-

A stubborn illusion

It starts with us

End with us

For us

Sometimes it's just a fuss

Not for long though

A long unknown fantasy

Or just a hallucinating reality

We don't know

What it is.

An artist:-

He was thinking alone

In his little cottage

About something new

Something out of my imagination range

Well a blessing in disguise

He had been cursed with

Such that no one could understand his art

But everyone enjoyed seeing it.

That night:-

I wasn't awake that night

Nor I was asleep

Still I could see the world

It was so deep

Its colours blinded me

Its unfamiliar face

Added to its creepiness

But I liked that new space

And then I saw another world

That I my self was aware of

Its colours were so old and bold

That I myself was bored of

Sure, there was gold

But it's darkening shine

Always added to a disgrace

But For this world's alpine

I couldn't catch her footpace

The blues:-

They are so colourful

With So many residents

They are beautiful

Just like the famous monuments

Although just a colour

They're light refracted into many

They're true glamour

Added to they're infinity

Then I saw

The inhabitants of the blues

With they're unknown laws

About whom I long didn't find any clues.

Tears:-

They lack sweetness

They are sour

But sometimes they are our happiness

An sometimes our dishonour

Well, a flow of emotions

We don't have a control on

So many irritations

We can conquer on.

Falling down:-

I was falling from the sky

It was so real

It was so high

Just as parallel

I then just popped out of no where

Into another sky

It was deep blue in colour

Just as it was pink .

Singing all alone:-

I saw him going the street

All alone

With his little feet

Singing all alone

He wasn't alive

Nor was he dead

Just like a lonely dive

Still un-dead

He was Singing his dreams out

In a swing

Such a peaceful layout

With a pensive tuning .

A dream's comet:-

It was like a sudden scratch

Through the sky's blue patch

As green as a spinach

It was just a death watch

Of a hundred dreams

That I wanted to wish

But I couldn't

Because of its swift vanish .

Light in darkness:-

I saw a blind person

He was crossing the road

So confident, although he was blind

Even many of us aren't that assertive

Maybe that person wasn't that blind

We all are

For us, vision's the cause of various visions

For him, his blindness added up to his confidence.

A spectrum of colours:-

A spectrum of colours

In that curved glance

Has changed my mood

For such an expanse

That I forgot reality

And was left in dreams

For a clarity

About the nature's daydreams.

Check out the Kindle version !!!!!!!!!!!!!!!!!!!!

****

Contents